@Copyright 2020by Diane Colby- **All rights reserved.**

This document is geared towards providing exact and reliable information in regards to the topic and issue covered. The publication is sold with the idea that the publisher is not required to render accounting, officially permitted, or otherwise, qualified services. If advice is necessary, legal or professional, a practiced individual in the profession should be ordered.

Under no circumstance will any legal responsibility or blame be held against the publisher for any reparation, damages, or monetary loss due to the information herein, either directly or indirectly.

Legal Notice: The book is copyright protected. This is only for personal use. You cannot amend, distribute, sell, use, quote or paraphrase any part or the content within this book without the consent of the author.

Disclaimer Notice: Please note the information contained within this document is for educational and entertainment purposes only. Every attempt has been made to provide accurate, up to date and reliable complete information. No warranties of any kind are expressed or implied. Readers acknowledge that the author is not engaging in the rendering of legal, financial, medical or professional advice. The content of this book has been derived from various sources. Please consult a licensed professional before attempting any techniques outlined in this book.

CONTENTS

Chapter 1: Breakfast 4
    Tomato And Bacon Morning Omelet 4
    Creative Potato Pancakes 5
    Grilled Up Maple Flavored Broccoli 6
    Plate-O-Bagels 7
    Original French Pineapple Toast 8
    Cool Potato Pancakes 9
    Early Morning Bacon Egg Muffins 10
    Airy Mac And Cheese 11
    Magical Sausage And Kale 12
    Blister Green Beans 13

Chapter 2: Delicious Poultry Recipes 14
    Alfredo Flavored Apple Chicken 14
    Maple Flavored Chicken 15
    Classic Chicken Tomatina 16
    Chicken Chili And Beans 17
    Hearty Chicken Tomatina 18
    Orange Flavored Chicken Fiesta 19
    Thai Baked Soy Chicken 20
    Seasoned Turkey Cutlets 21
    Soy Flavored Thai Chicken 22
    Tomato And Turkey Meal 23
    Zucchini And Chicken Kabobs 24

Chapter 3: Vegetable Recipes 25
    Mustard Dredged Veggie Delight 25
    Fruit Packed Lime Salad 26
    Corn And Mayo 27
    Asparagus Cream Soup 28
    Squash Leek Soup 29

    Keto Mushroom Tofu 30
    Charred up Shishito Pepper 31
    Corny Creamy Potatoes 32
    Arugula and Broccoli Meal 33
    The Creamy Potato Meal 34

Chapter 4: Beef And Pork Recipes 35
    Original Korean Pork 35
    Traditional Avocado Grill Salad 36
    All-Time Pineapple Steak 37
    Rosemary Anchovy Lamb 38
    Rosemary And Gold Potatoes Chop 39
    Authentic Asian Apple Steak 40
    Lamb And Garlic Sauce 41
    Chimichurri Sauce Steak 42
    Fine Onion Roasted Beef 43
    Green Pesto Ala Beef 44
    Bourbon Flavored Pork Chops 45

Chapter 5: Fish And Seafood Recipes 46
    Mustard-y Crisped Up Cod 46
    Daring Spicy Grilled Shrimp 47
    Awesome Shrimp Roast 48
    Salmon And Dill Sauce Meal 49
    Spicy Cajun Shrimp 50
    Subtly Roasted BBQ Shrimp 51
    Coho Glazed Salmon 52
    Swordfish With Caper Sauce 53

Chapter 6: Desserts 54
    Rummy Pineapple Sunday 54
    Marshmallow Banana Boat 55

    Fiery Cajun Eggplant Dish 56
    Granola Flavored Healthy Muffin 57
Chapter 7: Snacks And Appetizers Recipes 58
    Summer Squash With Garlic 58
Italian Oregano Squash 59
Elegant Pumpkin Seeds 60
Hearty Banana Fritters 61
Cool Avocado Fries 62
Fully Seasoned Broccoli Delight 63

Chapter 1: Breakfast

Tomato And Bacon Morning Omelet

Prep Time: 10 minutes
Cooking Time: 10 minutes
Number of Servings: 4

Ingredients:

- 4 whole eggs, whisked
- 1 tablespoon cheddar, grated
- ¼ pound bacon, cooked and chopped
- 4 tomatoes, cubed
- 1 tablespoon parsley, chopped
- 1 tablespoon olive oil
- Salt and pepper to taste

Method:

1. Take a small pan and place it over medium heat, add bacon and Sauté for 2 minutes until crisp
2. Take a bowl and add bacon, add remaining ingredients, and gently stir. Sprinkle cheese on top
3. Preheat Ninja Foodi by pressing the "BAKE" option and setting it to "400 Degrees F" and timer to 10 minutes
4. Let it preheat until you hear a beep
5. Pour mixture into a baking dish and transfer baking dish inside Ninja Foodi Grill, let it bake for 8 minutes
6. Serve and enjoy!

Nutritional Values (Per Serving)

Calories: 311 Fat: 16 g Saturated Fat: 4 g Carbohydrates: 23 g Fiber: 4 g Sodium: 149 mg Protein: 22 g

Creative Potato Pancakes

Prep Time: 10 minutes
Cooking Time: 24 minutes
Number of Servings: 4

Ingredients:

- 4 medium potatoes, peeled and cleaned
- 1 medium onion, chopped
- 1 beaten egg
- ¼ cup milk
- 2 tablespoons unsalted butter
- ½ teaspoon garlic powder
- ¼ teaspoon salt
- 3 tablespoons all-purpose flour
- Pepper as needed

Method:

1. Peel your potatoes and shred them up
2. Soak the shredded potatoes under cold water to remove starch
3. Drain the potatoes
4. Take a bowl and add eggs, milk, butter, garlic powder, salt, and pepper
5. Add in flour
6. Mix well
7. Add the shredded potatoes
8. Preheat Ninja Foodi by pressing the "AIR CRISP" option and setting it to "390 Degrees F" and timer to 24 minutes
9. let it preheat until you hear a beep
10. Add ¼ cup of the potato pancake batter to your cooking basket and cook for 12 minutes until the golden-brown texture is seen
11. Enjoy!

<u>Nutritional Values (Per Serving)</u>

Calories: 240 Fat: 11 g Saturated Fat: 4 g Carbohydrates: 33 g Fiber: 2 g Sodium: 259 mg Protein: 6

Grilled Up Maple Flavored Broccoli

Prep Time: 5-10 minutes
Cooking Time: 10 minutes
Number of Servings: 4

Ingredients:
- 2 heads broccoli, cut into florets
- 4 tablespoons soy sauce
- 2 tablespoons canola oil
- 4 tablespoons balsamic vinegar
- 2 teaspoons maple syrup
- Red pepper flakes and sesame seeds for garnish

Method:
1. Take a mixing bowl and add soy sauce, balsamic vinegar, oil, maple syrup and whisk well
2. Add broccoli and let it sit
3. Take your Ninja Foodi Grill and press "GRILL" and set to "MAX" mode, set the timer to 10 minutes
4. Let it preheat
5. Once you hear the beat, add broccoli over the grill grate
6. Lock lid and cook until the timer reads zero
7. Serve and enjoy with a topping of pepper flakes and sesame seeds

<u>Nutritional Values (Per Serving)</u>
Calories: 141 Fat: 7 g Saturated Fat: 1 g Carbohydrates: 14 g Fiber: 4 g Sodium: 853 mg Protein: 4 g

Plate-O-Bagels

Prep Time: 5-10 minutes
Cooking Time: 8 minutes
Number of Servings: 4

Ingredients:
- 1 cup fine sugar
- 2 tablespoons black coffee, prepared and cooled down
- 4 bagels, halved
- ¼ cup of coconut milk
- 2 tablespoons coconut flakes

Method:
1. Take your Ninja Foodi Grill and open lid, arrange grill grate and close top
2. Preheat Ninja Foodi by pressing the "GRILL" option and setting it to "MEDIUM" and timer to 8 minutes
3. let it preheat until you hear a beep
4. Arrange bagels over grill grate, lock lid and cook for 2 minutes, flip sausages and cook for 2 minutes more
5. Grill remaining Bagels similarly
6. Take a mixing bowl and mix remaining ingredients, pour the sauce over grilled bagels
7. Serve and enjoy!

Nutritional Values (Per Serving)
Calories: 300 Fat: 23 g Saturated Fat: 12 g Carbohydrates: 42 g Fiber: 4 g Sodium: 340 mg Protein: 18 g

Original French Pineapple Toast

Prep Time: 5-10 minutes
Cooking Time: 15 minutes
Number of Servings: 4

Ingredients:
- 10 bread slices
- ¼ cup of sugar
- ¼ cup milk
- 3 large whole eggs
- 1 cup of coconut milk
- 10 slices pineapple, peeled
- ½ cup coconut flakes
- Cooking spray as needed

Method:
1. Take a mixing bowl and whisk in coconut milk, sugar, eggs, milk and stir well
2. Dup breads in the mixture and keep the mon the side for 2 minutes
3. Pre-heat Ninja Foodi by pressing the "GRILL" option and setting it to "MED" and timer to 15 minutes
4. Let it pre-heat until you hear a beep
5. Arrange bread slices over grill grate, lock lid and cook for 2 minutes. Flip and cook for 2 minutes more, let them cook until the timer reads 0
6. Repeat with remaining slices, serve and enjoy!

Nutritional Values (Per Serving)
Calories: 202 Fat: 15 g Saturated Fat: 3 g Carbohydrates: 49 g Fiber: 3 g Sodium: 524 mg Protein: 8 g

Cool Potato Pancakes

Prep Time: 10 minutes
Cooking Time: 24 minutes
Number of Servings: 4

Ingredients:

- 4 medium potatoes, peeled and cleaned
- 1 medium onion, chopped
- 1 beaten egg
- ¼ cup milk
- 2 tablespoons unsalted butter
- ½ teaspoon garlic powder
- ¼ teaspoon salt
- 3 tablespoons all-purpose flour
- Pepper as needed

Method:
1. Peel your potatoes and shred them up
2. Soak the shredded potatoes under cold water to remove starch
3. Drain the potatoes
4. Take a bowl and add eggs, milk, butter, garlic powder, salt, and pepper
5. Add in flour
6. Mix well
7. Add the shredded potatoes
8. Pre-heat Ninja Foodi by pressing the "AIR CRISP" option and setting it to "390 Degrees F" and timer to 24 minutes
9. let it pre-heat until you hear a beep
10. Add ¼ cup of the potato pancake batter to your cooking basket and cook for 12 minutes until the golden-brown texture is seen
11. Enjoy!

<u>Nutritional Values (Per Serving)</u>

Calories: 240 Fat: 11 g Saturated Fat: 4 g Carbohydrates: 33 g Fiber: 2 g Sodium: 259 mg Protein: 6 g

Early Morning Bacon Egg Muffins

Prep Time: 5 minutes
Cooking Time: 7-10 minutes
Number of Servings: 4

Ingredients:
- 1 whole egg
- 2 streaky bacon
- 1 English muffin
- Salt and pepper to taste

Method:
1. Pre-heat Ninja Foodi by pressing the "AIR CRISP" option and setting it to "200 Degrees F" and timer to 10 minutes
2. let it pre-heat until you hear a beep
3. Take an ovenproof bowl and crack in an egg
4. Take Ninja Foodi cooking basket and add bacon, egg, and muffin into Fryer
5. Cook for 7 mutes
6. Assemble muffin done by packing bacon and egg on top of English muffin
7. Serve and enjoy!

Nutritional Values (Per Serving)

Calories: 600 Fat: 40 g Saturated Fat: 10 g Carbohydrates: 30 g Fiber: 5 g Sodium: 526 mg Protein: 24 g

Airy Mac And Cheese

Prep Time: 10 minutes
Cooking Time: 10 minutes
Number of Servings: 4

Ingredients:
- 1 cup elbow macaroni
- ½ cup broccoli
- ½ cup warmed milk
- 1 and ½ cheddar cheese, grated
- Salt and pepper to taste
- 1 tablespoon parmesan cheese, grated

Method:
1. Pre-heat Ninja Foodi by pressing the "AIR CRISP" option and setting it to "400 Degrees F" and timer to 10 minutes
2. let it pre-heat until you hear a beep
3. Take a pot and add water, allow it to boil
4. Add macaroni and veggies and broil for about 10 minutes until the mixture is Al Dente
5. Drain the pasta and vegetables
6. Toss the pasta and veggies with cheese
7. Season with some pepper and salt and transfer the mixture to your Foodi
8. Sprinkle some more parmesan on top and cook for about 15 minutes.
9. Allow it to cool for about 10 minutes once done
10. Enjoy!

Nutritional Values (Per Serving)

Calories: 180 Fat: 11 g Saturated Fat: 3 g Carbohydrates: 14 g Fiber: 2 g Sodium: 147 mg Protein: 6 g

Magical Sausage And Kale

Prep Time: 10 minutes
Cooking Time: 10 minutes
Number of Servings: 4

Ingredients:
- 1 medium sweet yellow onion
- 4 medium eggs
- 4 sausage links
- 2 cups kale, chopped
- 1 cup mushrooms
- Olive oil as needed

Method:
1. Take your Ninja Foodi Grill and open lid, arrange grill grate and close top
2. Preheat Ninja Foodi by pressing the "GRILL" option and setting it to "HIGH" and timer to 5 minutes
3. let it preheat until you hear a beep
4. Arrange sausages over grill grate, lock lid and cook for 2 minutes, flip sausages and cook for 3 minutes more
5. Take sausages out
6. Take a baking pan and spread onion, kale, mushrooms, sausages and crack eggs on top
7. Arrange pan inside the grill and used the "BAKE" option to bake it at 350 degrees F for 5 minutes
8. Once done, open lid and serve
9. Enjoy!

<u>Nutritional Values (Per Serving)</u>

Calories: 236 Fat: 12 g Saturated Fat: 2 g Carbohydrates: 17 g Fiber: 4 g Sodium: 369 mg Protein: 18 g

Blister Green Beans

Prep Time: 5 minutes
Cooking Time: 10 minutes
Number of Servings: 4

Ingredients:
- 1-pound green beans, trimmed
- 2 tablespoons vegetable oil
- 1 lemon, juiced
- Pinch of red pepper flakes
- Flaky sea salt as needed
- Fresh ground black pepper as needed

Method:
1. Take a medium-sized bowl and add green beans
2. Preheat Ninja Foodi by pressing the "GRILL" option and setting it to "MAX" and timer to 10 minutes
3. Let it preheat until you hear a beep
4. Once preheated, transfer green beans to Grill Grate
5. Lock lid and let them grill for 8-10 minutes, making sure to toss them from time to time until all sides are blustered well
6. Squeeze lemon juice over green beans and top with red pepper flakes, season with salt and pepper

<u>Nutritional Values (Per Serving)</u>

Calories: 100 Fat: 7 g Saturated Fat: 1 g Carbohydrates: 10 g Fiber: 4 g Sodium: 30 mg Protein: 2 g

Chapter 2: Delicious Poultry Recipes

Alfredo Flavored Apple Chicken

Prep Time: 5-10 minutes **Number of Servings: 4**
Cooking Time: 20 minutes

Ingredients:
- 1 large apple, wedged
- 1 tablespoon lemon juice
- 4 chicken breast, halved
- 4 teaspoon chicken seasoning
- 4 slices provolone cheese
- ¼ cup blue cheese, crumbled
- ½ cup alfredo sauce

Method:
1. Take a bowl and add chicken, season it well
2. Take another bowl and add in apple, lemon juice
3. Preheat Ninja Foodi by pressing the "GRILL" option and setting it to "MED" and timer to 20 minutes
4. Let it preheat until you hear a beep
5. Arrange chicken over Grill Grate, lock lid and cook for 8 minutes, flip and cook for 8 minutes more
6. Grill apple in the same manner for 2 minutes per side (making sure to remove chicken beforehand)
7. Serve chicken with pepper, apple, blue cheese, and alfredo sauce
8. Enjoy!

Nutritional Values (Per Serving)
Calories: 247 Fat: 19 g Saturated Fat: 6 g Carbohydrates: 29 g Fiber: 6 g Sodium: 853 mg Protein: 14 g

Maple Flavored Chicken

Prep Time: 5-10 minutes
Cooking Time: 15 minutes
Number of Servings: 4

Ingredients:
- 3 garlic cloves, minced
- 2 teaspoons garlic powder
- 2 teaspoons onion powder
- 1 teaspoon pepper
- ¼ cup teriyaki sauce
- 1 cup maple syrup
- 1/3 cup soy sauce
- 2 pounds bone-in chicken wings

Method:
1. Take a mixing bowl and add soy sauce, pepper, onion powder, garlic, maple syrup, garlic powder, teriyaki sauce and combine well
2. Add chicken wings to the mixture and coat well
3. Preheat Ninja Foodi by pressing the "GRILL" option and setting it to "MED" and timer to 12 minutes
4. Let it preheat until you hear a beep
5. Arrange wings over grill grate and let it cook for 5 minutes, flip the wings and cook for 5 minutes more
6. Once the internal temperature reaches 165 degrees F, grill for 3-4 minutes more
7. Serve and enjoy!

Nutritional Values (Per Serving)

Calories: 520 Fat: 26 g Saturated Fat: 8 g Carbohydrates: 40 g Fiber: 3 g Sodium: 1400 mg Protein: 42 g

Classic Chicken Tomatina

Prep Time: 5-10 minutes

Cooking Time: 12 minutes

Number of Servings: 4

Ingredients:
- 4 chicken breast, boneless and skinless
- ¼ cup fresh basil leaves
- 8 plum tomatoes
- 3/4 cup vinegar
- 2 tablespoons olive oil
- 1 garlic clove, minced
- ½ teaspoon salt

Method:
1. Take your food processor and add basil, vinegar, olive oil, salt, garlic and blend until smooth
2. Add tomatoes and blend again
3. Take a mixing bowl and add chicken, tomato mixture and mix well, let it chill for 1-2 hours
4. Preheat Ninja Foodi by pressing the "GRILL" option and setting it to "HIGH" and timer to 6 minutes
5. Let it preheat until you hear a beep
6. Arrange prepared chicken over grill grate, lock lid and let it cook for 3 minutes
7. Flip chicken and cook for 3 minutes more, serve and enjoy!

<u>Nutritional Values (Per Serving)</u>
Calories: 400 Fat: 5 g Saturated Fat: 3 g Carbohydrates: 18 g Fiber: 3 g Sodium: 230 mg Protein: 23 g

Chicken Chili And Beans

Prep Time: 10 minutes

Cooking Time: 15 minutes

Number of Servings: 4

Ingredients:
- 1 and ¼ pounds chicken breast, cut into pieces
- 1 can corn
- ¼ teaspoon garlic powder
- 1 can black beans, drained and rinsed
- 1 tablespoon oil
- 2 tablespoons chili powder
- 1 bell pepper, chopped
- ¼ teaspoon garlic powder
- ¼ teaspoon salt

Method:
1. Pre-heat Ninja Foodi by pressing the "AIR CRISP" option and setting it to "360 Degrees F" and timer to 15 minutes
2. Place all the ingredients in your Ninja Foodi Grill cooking basket/alternatively, you may use a dish to mix the ingredients and then put the dish in the cooking basket
3. Stir to mix well
4. Cook for 15 minutes
5. Serve and enjoy!

<u>Nutritional Values (Per Serving)</u>
Calories: 220 Fat: 4 g Saturated Fat: 1 g Carbohydrates: 24 g Fiber: 2 g Sodium: 856 mg Protein: 20 g

Hearty Chicken Tomatina

Prep Time: 5-10 minutes

Cooking Time: 12 minutes

Number of Servings: 4

Ingredients:
- 4 chicken breast, boneless and skinless
- ¼ cup fresh basil leaves
- 8 plum tomatoes
- 3/4 cup vinegar
- 2 tablespoons olive oil
- 1 garlic clove, minced
- ½ teaspoon salt

Method:
1. Take your food processor and add basil, vinegar, olive oil, salt, garlic and blend until smooth
2. Add tomatoes and blend again
3. Take a mixing bowl and add chicken, tomato mixture and mix well, let it chill for 1-2 hours
4. Pre-heat Ninja Foodi by pressing the "GRILL" option and setting it to "HIGH" and timer to 12 minutes
5. Let it pre-heat until you hear a beep
6. Arrange prepared chicken over grill grate, lock lid and let it cook for 3 minutes
7. Flip chicken and cook for 3 minutes more, serve and enjoy!

<u>Nutritional Values (Per Serving)</u>

Calories: 400 Fat: 5 g Saturated Fat: 1 g Carbohydrates: 18 g Fiber: 3 g Sodium: 230 mg Protein: 23 g

Orange Flavored Chicken Fiesta

Prep Time: 5-10 minutes
Cooking Time: 10 minutes
Number of Servings: 5

Ingredients:
- 2 teaspoons coriander, ground
- ½ teaspoon garlic salt
- ¼ teaspoon black pepper
- 12 chicken wings
- 1 tablespoon canola oil

Sauce
- ¼ cup butter
- 3 tablespoons honey
- ½ cup orange juice
- 1/3 cup Sriracha chili sauce
- 2 tablespoons lime juice
- ¼ cup cilantro, chopped

Method:
1. Take your chicken and coat with oil, season well with spices and let it chill for 2 hours
2. Take a bowl and add sauce ingredients, mix well. Stir cook for 3-4 minutes
3. Set you Ninja Foodi to GRILL mode and select MED, adjust the timer to 10 minutes
4. Let it preheat until you hear a beep
5. Arrange chicken over grill, lock lid and cook for 5 minutes, flip and cook for 5 minutes more
6. Serve and enjoy!

Nutritional Values (Per Serving)
Calories: 327 Fat: 14 g Saturated Fat: 3 g Carbohydrates: 19 g Fiber: 1 g Sodium: 258 mg Protein: 25 g

Thai Baked Soy Chicken

Prep Time: 5-10 minutes
Cooking Time: 25 minutes
Number of Servings: 5

Ingredients:

- ½ cup of soy sauce
- ¼ cup apple cider vinegar
- 1 garlic clove, minced
- 1 tablespoon cornstarch
- 1 tablespoon cold water
- ½ cup white sugar
- ¼ teaspoon ground pepper
- ½ teaspoon ground ginger
- 12 skinless chicken thighs

Method:

1. Take a mixing bowl and add cornstarch water, white sugar, soy sauce, apple cider, vinegar, garlic, ginger, and pepper, mix and combine well
2. Season chicken with salt and pepper
3. Take your cooking pan and grease well with oil, add chicken and soy sauce mix on top
4. Preheat Ninja Foodi by pressing the "BAKE" option and setting it to "350 degrees F" and timer to 25 minutes
5. Let it preheat until you hear a beep
6. Arrange the pan over grill grate, lock lid and let it cook until the timer goes to zero
7. Serve and enjoy!

Nutritional Values (Per Serving)

Calories: 570 Fat: 19 g Saturated Fat: 5 g Carbohydrates: 23 g Fiber: 1 g Sodium: 600 mg Protein: 40 g

Seasoned Turkey Cutlets

Prep Time: 5-10 min.
Cooking Time: 22 min.
Number of Servings: 4

Ingredients:
- 2 tablespoons olive oil
- 1 teaspoon turmeric powder
- ½ cup almond flour
- 1 teaspoon Greek seasoning
- 1 pound turkey cutlets

Method:
1. In a mixing bowl, add the Greek seasoning, turmeric powder, and almond flour. Combine the ingredients to mix well with each other. Add the turkey cutlets and coat well; set aside for 30 minutes.
2. Take Ninja Foodi multi-cooker, arrange it over a cooking platform, and open the top lid.
3. In the pot, add the oil; Select "SEAR/SAUTÉ" mode and select "MD: HI" pressure level. Press "STOP/START." After about 4-5 minutes, the oil will start simmering.
4. Add the cutlets and stir-cook for about 2-3 minutes to brown evenly.
5. Seal the multi-cooker by locking it with the pressure lid; ensure to keep the pressure release valve locked/sealed.
6. Select "PRESSURE" mode and select the "LOW: MD" pressure level. Then, set timer to 20 minutes and press "STOP/START"; it will start the cooking process by building up inside pressure.
7. When the timer goes off, naturally release inside pressure for about 8-10 minutes. Then, quick-release pressure by adjusting the pressure valve to the VENT. Serve warm.

Nutritional Values (Per Serving):
Calories: 355 Fat: 18.5g Saturated Fat: 1g Trans Fat: 0g Carbohydrates: 4g Fiber: 0.5g Sodium: 544mg Protein: 35g

Soy Flavored Thai Chicken

Prep Time: 5-10 minutes
Cooking Time: 25 minutes
Number of Servings: 5

Ingredients:

- ½ cup of soy sauce
- ¼ cup apple cider vinegar
- 1 garlic clove, minced
- 1 tablespoon cornstarch
- 1 tablespoon cold water
- ½ cup white sugar
- ¼ teaspoon ground pepper
- ½ teaspoon ground ginger
- 12 skinless chicken thighs

Method:

1. Take a mixing bowl and add cornstarch water, white sugar, soy sauce, apple cider, vinegar, garlic, ginger, and pepper, mix and combine well
2. Season chicken with salt and pepper
3. Take your cooking pan and grease well with oil, add chicken and soy sauce mix on top
4. Preheat Ninja Foodi by pressing the "BAKE" option and setting it to "350 degrees F" and timer to 25 minutes
5. Let it preheat until you hear a beep
6. Arrange the pan over grill grate, lock lid and let it cook until the timer goes to zero
7. Serve and enjoy!

<u>Nutritional Values (Per Serving)</u>

Calories: 570 Fat: 19 g Saturated Fat: 5 g Carbohydrates: 23 g Fiber: 1 g Sodium: 600 mg Protein: 40 g

Soy Flavored Thai Chicken

Prep Time: 5-10 minutes
Cooking Time: 25 minutes
Number of Servings: 5

Ingredients:

- ½ cup of soy sauce
- ¼ cup apple cider vinegar
- 1 garlic clove, minced
- 1 tablespoon cornstarch
- 1 tablespoon cold water
- ½ cup white sugar
- ¼ teaspoon ground pepper
- ½ teaspoon ground ginger
- 12 skinless chicken thighs

Method:

1. Take a mixing bowl and add cornstarch water, white sugar, soy sauce, apple cider, vinegar, garlic, ginger, and pepper, mix and combine well
2. Season chicken with salt and pepper
3. Take your cooking pan and grease well with oil, add chicken and soy sauce mix on top
4. Preheat Ninja Foodi by pressing the "BAKE" option and setting it to "350 degrees F" and timer to 25 minutes
5. Let it preheat until you hear a beep
6. Arrange the pan over grill grate, lock lid and let it cook until the timer goes to zero
7. Serve and enjoy!

Nutritional Values (Per Serving)

Calories: 570 Fat: 19 g Saturated Fat: 5 g Carbohydrates: 23 g Fiber: 1 g Sodium: 600 mg Protein: 40 g

Seasoned Turkey Cutlets

Prep Time: 5-10 min.
Cooking Time: 22 min.
Number of Servings: 4

Ingredients:

- 2 tablespoons olive oil
- 1 teaspoon turmeric powder
- ½ cup almond flour
- 1 teaspoon Greek seasoning
- 1 pound turkey cutlets

Method:

1. In a mixing bowl, add the Greek seasoning, turmeric powder, and almond flour. Combine the ingredients to mix well with each other. Add the turkey cutlets and coat well; set aside for 30 minutes.
2. Take Ninja Foodi multi-cooker, arrange it over a cooking platform, and open the top lid.
3. In the pot, add the oil; Select "SEAR/SAUTÉ" mode and select "MD: HI" pressure level. Press "STOP/START." After about 4-5 minutes, the oil will start simmering.
4. Add the cutlets and stir-cook for about 2-3 minutes to brown evenly.
5. Seal the multi-cooker by locking it with the pressure lid; ensure to keep the pressure release valve locked/sealed.
6. Select "PRESSURE" mode and select the "LOW: MD" pressure level. Then, set timer to 20 minutes and press "STOP/START"; it will start the cooking process by building up inside pressure.
7. When the timer goes off, naturally release inside pressure for about 8-10 minutes. Then, quick-release pressure by adjusting the pressure valve to the VENT. Serve warm.

Nutritional Values (Per Serving):

Calories: 355 Fat: 18.5g Saturated Fat: 1g Trans Fat: 0g Carbohydrates: 4g Fiber: 0.5g Sodium: 544mg Protein: 35g

Tomato And Turkey Meal

Prep Time: 10 minutes
Cooking Time: 40 minutes
Number of Servings: 4

Ingredients:
- 3 ounces plain granola
- 2 pounds lean turkey, grounded
- 6 burger buns of your choice, sliced in half
- 2/3 cup sun-dried tomatoes, chopped
- 1 cup feta cheese, crumbled
- ¼ teaspoon salt
- ¼ teaspoon pepper
- 1 large red onion, chopped

Method:
1. Take a mixing bowl, add all the ingredients and combine them well
2. Prepare six patties from the mixture
3. Arrange the grill grate and close the lid
4. Preheat Ninja Foodi by pressing the "GRILL" option and setting it to "MED" and timer to 14 minutes
5. Let it preheat until you hear a beep
6. Arrange the patties over the grill grate, lock lid and cook for 7 minutes more
7. Serve warm with ciabatta rolls and your favorite toppings
8. Enjoy!

Nutritional Values (Per Serving)
Calories: 298 Fat: 16 g Saturated Fat: 4 g Carbohydrates: 32 g Fiber: 4 g Sodium: 168 mg Protein: 27 g

Zucchini And Chicken Kabobs

Prep Time: 10 minutes
Cooking Time: 15 minutes
Number of Servings: 4

Ingredients:

- 1 pound chicken breast, boneless, skinless and cut into cubes of 2 inches
- 2 tablespoons Greek yogurt, plain
- 4 lemons juice
- 1 lemon zest
- ¼ cup extra-virgin olive oil
- 2 tablespoons oregano
- 1 red onion, quartered
- 1 zucchini, sliced
- 4 garlic cloves, minced
- 1 teaspoon of sea salt
- ½ teaspoon ground black pepper

Method:

1. Take a mixing bowl, add the Greek yogurt, lemon juice, oregano, garlic, zest, salt, and pepper, combine them well
2. Add the chicken and coat well, refrigerate for 1-2 hours to marinate
3. Arrange the grill grate and close the lid
4. Preheat Ninja Foodi by pressing the "GRILL" option and setting it to "MED" and timer to 7 minutes
5. Take the skewers, thread the chicken, zucchini and red onion and thread alternatively
6. Let it preheat until you hear a beep
7. Arrange the skewers over the grill grate, lock lid and cook until the timer reads zero
8. Baste the kebabs with a marinating mixture in between
9. Take out your when it reaches 165 degrees F
10. Serve warm and enjoy!

Nutritional Values (Per Serving)

Calories: 277 Fat: 15 g Saturated Fat: 4 g Carbohydrates: 10 g Fiber: 2 g Sodium: 146 mg Protein: 25 g

Chapter 3: Vegetable Recipes

Mustard Dredged Veggie Delight

Prep Time: 5-10 minutes
Cooking Time: 30-40 minutes
Number of Servings: 4

Ingredients:
Vinaigrette
- 2 tablespoons Dijon mustard
- ½ cup red wine vinegar
- 2 tablespoons honey
- 1 teaspoon salt
- ¼ teaspoon pepper
- ½ cup avocado oil
- ½ cup olive oil

Veggies
- 4 zucchinis, halved
- 4 sweet onion, quartered
- 4 red pepper, seeded and halved
- 2 bunch green onions, trimmed
- 4 yellow squash, cut in half

Method:
1. Take a small-sized bowl and whisk in vinegar, mustard, honey, pepper, and salt. Add oils and combine well to make a smooth mixture
2. Preheat Ninja Foodi by pressing the "GRILL" option and setting it to "MED" and timer to 40 minutes
3. Let it preheat until you hear a beep
4. Arrange the onion quarters over the Grill Grate, lock lid, and cook for 5 minutes. Flip onions and cook for 5 minutes more
5. Grill remaining vegetables similarly, giving 7 minutes per side for the zucchini and pepper, and 1 minute per side for green onions
6. Serve the grilled vegetables with the mustard vinaigrette on top
7. Enjoy!

Nutritional Values (Per Serving)
Calories: 327 Fat: 5 g Saturated Fat: 2 g Carbohydrates:328 g Fiber: 2 g Sodium: 524 mg Protein: 8 g

Fruit Packed Lime Salad

Prep Time: 5-10 minutes
Cooking Time: 4 minutes
Number of Servings: 4

Ingredients:
- ½ pound strawberries washed, hulled and halved
- 1 can (9 ounces) pineapple chunks, drained, juice reserved
- 2 peaches, pitted and sliced
- 6 tablespoons honey, divided
- 1 tablespoon freshly squeezed lime juice

Method:
1. Take a large bowl and add strawberries, pineapple, peaches, and 3 tablespoons, honey, toss well
2. Preheat Ninja Foodi by pressing the "GRILL" option and setting it to "MAX" and timer to 4 minutes
3. Let it preheat until you hear a beep
4. Transfer fruits to Grill Grate, lock lid and cook for 4 minutes
5. Take a small-sized bowl and add remaining 3 tablespoons of honey, lime juice, 1 tablespoon reserved pineapple juice
6. Once cooking is done, place fruits in a large-sized bowl and toss with honey mixture, serve and enjoy!

<u>Nutritional Values (Per Serving)</u>

Calories: 178 Fat: 1 g Saturated Fat: 0 g Carbohydrates:47 g Fiber: 3 g Sodium: 3 mg Protein: 2 g

Corn And Mayo

Prep Time: 5-10 minutes
Cooking Time: 12 minutes
Number of Servings: 4

Ingredients:
- 2 tablespoons plain yogurt
- 4 ears corn, husked
- ½ teaspoon chili powder
- 2 tablespoon mayonnaise
- 4 tablespoons finely shredded parmesan, cheese
- 1 lime, quartered

Method:
1. Take a mixing bowl and add yogurt, mayonnaise, chili powder, mix well
2. Take your Ninja Foodi Grill and press "GRILL" and set to "LOW" mode, set the timer to 12 minutes
3. Let it preheat
4. Once you hear a beep, arrange corn over the grill grate
5. Lock lid and cook for 6 minutes, flip and cook for 6 minutes more
6. Serve with prepared sauce, add cheese on top
7. Serve with warm lime wedges, enjoy!

Nutritional Values (Per Serving)
Calories: 286 Fat: 4 g Saturated Fat: 1 g Carbohydrates: 22 g Fiber: 6 g Sodium: 542 mg Protein: 4 g

Asparagus Cream Soup

Prep Time: 5-10 min.
Cooking Time: 5 min.
Number of Servings: 4

Ingredients:
- 1 pound asparagus, trimmed and cut into 1 inch pieces
- 4 cups vegetable stock
- 1 tablespoon olive oil
- 3 green onions, sliced crosswise
- 1 tablespoon almond flour
- 2 teaspoons salt
- 1 teaspoon white pepper
- 1 tablespoon unsalted full-fat butter, melted
- ½ cup heavy cream

Method:
1. Take Ninja Foodi multi-cooker, arrange it over a cooking platform, and open the top lid.
2. In the pot, add the oil; Select "SEAR/SAUTÉ" mode and select "MD: HI" pressure level. Press "STOP/START." After about 4-5 minutes, the oil will start simmering.
3. Add the onions and cook (while stirring) until they become softened and translucent. In the pot, add the stock and asparagus. Stir the mixture.
4. Seal the multi-cooker by locking it with the pressure lid; ensure to keep the pressure release valve locked/sealed.
5. Select "PRESSURE" mode and select the "HI" pressure level. Then, set timer to 5 minutes and press "STOP/START"; it will start the cooking process by building up inside pressure.
6. When the timer goes off, naturally release inside pressure for about 8-10 minutes. Then, quick-release pressure by adjusting the pressure valve to the VENT. After pressure gets released, open the pressure lid.
7. Mix in the flour mixture. Season to taste with black pepper and salt. Add the mixture in a blender and blend to make a puree.
8. Mix in the cream and serve warm.

Nutritional Values (Per Serving):
Calories: 203 Fat: 14.5g Saturated Fat: 3g Trans Fat: 0g Carbohydrates: 7.5g Fiber: 2g Sodium: 358mg Protein: 6g

Squash Leek Soup

Prep Time: 5-10 min.
Cooking Time: 6 min.
Number of Servings: 6

Ingredients:
- 1 cup celery, chopped
- 2 tablespoons garlic, minced
- 1 teaspoon dried oregano
- 3 cups leeks, sliced
- 6 cups rainbow chard, stemmed and chopped
- 1 teaspoon salt
- 2 teaspoons ground black pepper
- ¼ cup parsley, chopped
- ¾ cup heavy whip cream
- 4-6 tablespoons parmesan cheese, grated
- 3 cups chicken broth
- 2 cups yellow summer squash, sliced into 1/ inch slices

Method:
1. Take Ninja Foodi multi-cooker, arrange it over a cooking platform, and open the top lid.
2. In the pot, add the broth, leeks, chard, celery, 1 tablespoon garlic, oregano, salt, and black pepper. Stir the mixture.
3. Seal the multi-cooker by locking it with the pressure lid; ensure to keep the pressure release valve locked/sealed.
4. Select "PRESSURE" mode and select the "HI" pressure level. Then, set timer to 3 minutes and press "STOP/START"; it will start the cooking process by building up inside pressure.
5. When the timer goes off, quick release pressure by adjusting the pressure valve to the VENT. After pressure gets released, open the pressure lid.
6. Select "SEAR/SAUTÉ" mode and select the "MD" pressure level; add the yellow squash, parsley, and remaining 1 tablespoon garlic and combine. Stir-cook for 2-3 minutes.
7. Stir in the cream and parmesan. Serve warm.

Nutritional Values (Per Serving):
Calories: 258 Fat: 15.5g Saturated Fat: 4g Trans Fat: 0g Carbohydrates: 9g Fiber: 2.5g Sodium: 549mg Protein: 11g

Keto Mushroom Tofu

Prep Time: 5-10 min.
Cooking Time: 10 min.
Number of Servings: 2

Ingredients:

- 2 blocks tofu, pressed and cubed
- 8 tablespoons parmesan cheese, shredded
- 2 cups mushrooms, chopped
- Black pepper (ground) and salt to taste
- 8 tablespoons full-fat butter

Method:

1. In a mixing bowl, add the tofu, salt, and black pepper. Combine the ingredients to mix well with each other.
2. Take Ninja Foodi multi-cooker, arrange it over a cooking platform, and open the top lid.
3. In the pot, add the oil; Select "SEAR/SAUTÉ" mode and select "MD: HI" pressure level. Press "STOP/START." After about 4-5 minutes, the oil will start simmering.
4. Add the seasoned tofu and cook (while stirring) until it becomes softened for 4-5 minutes. Add the mushroom, cheese, and stir-cook for 3 minutes.
5. Seal the multi-cooker by locking it with the crisping lid; ensure to keep the pressure release valve locked/sealed.
6. Select the "AIR CRISP" mode and adjust the 350°F temperature level. Then, set timer to 3 minutes and press "STOP/START"; it will start the cooking process by building up inside pressure.
7. When the timer goes off, quick release pressure by adjusting the pressure valve to the VENT. After pressure gets released, open the crisping lid. Serve warm.

Nutritional Values (Per Serving):

Calories: 236 Fat: 11g Saturated Fat: 3g Trans Fat: 0g Carbohydrates: 2.5g Fiber: 0.5g Sodium: 447mg Protein: 11g

Charred up Shishito Pepper

Prep Time: 10 minutes
Cooking Time: 10 minutes
Number of Servings: 4

Ingredients:
- 3 cups Shishito peppers
- 2 tablespoons vegetable oil
- Salt and pepper to taste

Method:
1. Select GRILL mode and set your Ninja Foodi Grill to "MAX," set timer to 10 minutes
2. Let it preheat until you hear a beep
3. Transfer pepper to grill grate and press peppers down, lock lid and cook for 8-10 minutes
4. Once done, serve with some salt and pepper sprinkled on top
5. Enjoy!

Nutritional Values (Per Serving)
Calories: 83 Fat: 7 g Saturated Fat: 2 g Carbohydrates: 5 g Fiber: 1 g Sodium: 49 mg Protein: 2 g

Corny Creamy Potatoes

Prep Time: 5-10 minutes
Cooking Time: 30-40 minutes
Number of Servings: 4

Ingredients:

- 1 and ½ pound red potatoes, quartered and boiled
- 3 tablespoons olive oil
- 1 tablespoon cilantro, minced
- 2 sweet corn ears, without husks
- ¼ teaspoon cayenne pepper
- 2 poblano pepper
- ½ cup milk
- 1 teaspoon ground cumin
- 1 tablespoon lime juice
- 1 jalapeno pepper, seeded and minced
- ½ cup sour cream
- 1 and ½ teaspoon garlic salt

Method:

1. Drain the potatoes and rub them well with oil
2. Preheat Ninja Foodi by pressing the "GRILL" option and setting it to "MED" and timer to 10 minutes
3. Let it preheat until you hear a beep
4. Arrange your prepared poblano pepper over the grill grate, lock lid and cook for 5 minutes
5. Flip the peppers and cook for 5 minutes more
6. Grill the remaining vegetables in the same manner with 7 minutes each side for the potatoes and corn
7. Take a bowl and whisk in remaining ingredients to prepare the vinaigrette
8. Peel the grilled corn and chop
9. Divide corn ears into small pieces and cut your potatoes
10. Serve the grilled veggies with the vinaigrette topping
11. Enjoy!

Nutritional Values (Per Serving)

Calories: 344 Fat: 5 g Saturated Fat: 1 g Carbohydrates: 51 g Fiber: 3 g Sodium: 600 mg Protein: 5 g

Arugula and Broccoli Meal

Prep Time: 10 minutes
Cooking Time: 12 minutes
Number of Servings: 4

Ingredients:

- 2 heads broccoli, trimmed into florets
- 4 cups arugula, torn
- 2 tablespoons parmesan cheese, grated
- 1 tablespoon lemon juice
- 1 teaspoon honey
- 1 teaspoon Dijon mustard
- 1 garlic cloves, minced
- ½ red onion, sliced
- 1 tablespoon canola oil
- 2 tablespoons extra-virgin olive oil
- Red pepper flakes
- ¼ teaspoon of sea salt
- Black pepper, freshly grounded

Method:

1. Insert the grill grate and close the hood
2. Preheat Ninja Foodi by pressing the "GRILL" option at and setting it to "MAX" and timer to 12 minutes
3. Take a large bowl and combine the broccoli, sliced onions, canola oil
4. Toss until coated
5. Once it preheats until you hear a beep
6. Arrange the vegetables over the grill grate, lock lid and cook for 8 to 12 minutes
7. Take a medium bowl and whisk together lemon juice, mustard, olive oil, honey, garlic, red pepper flakes, salt, and pepper
8. Once cooked, combine the roasted vegetables and arugula in a large serving bowl
9. Drizzle with the vinaigrette to taste and sprinkle with parmesan cheese
10. Serve and enjoy!

Nutritional Values (Per Serving)

Calories: 168 Fat: 12 g Saturated Fat: 3 g Carbohydrates: 13 g Fiber: 1 g Sodium: 392 mg Protein: 6 g

The Creamy Potato Meal

Prep Time: 10 minutes
Cooking Time: 30- 40 minutes
Number of Servings: 4

Ingredients:
- 1 and ½ pound red potatoes, quartered and boiled
- 3 tablespoons olive oil
- 1 tablespoon cilantro, minced
- 2 sweet corn ears, without husks
- ¼ teaspoon cayenne pepper
- 2 poblano pepper
- ½ cup milk
- 1 teaspoon ground cumin
- 1 tablespoon lime juice
- 1 jalapeno pepper, seeded and minced
- ½ cup sour cream
- 1 and ½ teaspoon garlic salt

Method:
1. Drain the potatoes and rub them well with oil
2. Preheat Ninja Foodi by pressing the "GRILL" option and setting it to "MED" and timer to 10 minutes
3. Let it preheat until you hear a beep
4. Arrange your prepared poblano pepper over the grill grate, lock lid and cook for 5 minutes
5. Flip the peppers and cook for 5 minutes more
6. Grill the remaining vegetables in the same manner with 7 minutes each side for the potatoes and corn
7. Take a bowl and whisk in remaining ingredients to prepare the vinaigrette
8. Peel the grilled corn and chop
9. Divide corn ears into small pieces and cut your potatoes
10. Serve the grilled veggies with the vinaigrette topping
11. Enjoy!

Nutritional Values (Per Serving)
Calories: 344 Fat: 5 g Saturated Fat: 1 g Carbohydrates: 31 g Fiber: 5 g Sodium: 96 mg Protein: 5 g

Chapter 4: Beef And Pork Recipes

Original Korean Pork

Prep Time: 5-10 minutes
Cooking Time: 8 minutes
Number of Servings: 4

Ingredients:
- 2 pounds pork, cut into 1/8-inch slices
- 5 garlic cloves, minced
- 3 tablespoons green onion, minced
- 1 yellow onion, sliced
- ½ cup of soy sauce
- ½ cup brown sugar
- 3 tablespoons Korean Red Chili Paste
- 2 tablespoons sesame seeds
- 3 teaspoons black pepper
- Red pepper flakes

Method:
1. Take a zip bag and add listed ingredients, shake well and let it chill for 6-8 hours
2. Preheat Ninja Foodi by pressing the "GRILL" option and setting it to "MED" and timer to 8 minutes
3. Let it preheat until you hear a beep
4. Arrange sliced pork over grill grate, lock lid and cook for 4 minutes
5. Flip pork and cook for 4 minutes more, serve warm and enjoy with some chopped lettuce

Nutritional Values (Per Serving)
Calories: 621 Fat: 31 g Saturated Fat: 12 g Carbohydrates: 29 g Fiber: 3 g Sodium: 1428 mg Protein: 53 g

Traditional Avocado Grill Salad

Prep Time: 5-10 minutes

Cooking Time: 18 minutes

Number of Servings: 4

Ingredients:

- 1 cup cilantro leaves
- 2 ripe avocados, diced
- 2 cups salsa Verde
- 2 beef lank steak, diced
- ½ teaspoon salt
- ½ teaspoon pepper
- 2 medium tomatoes, seeded and diced

Method:

1. Rub beef steak with salt and pepper, season well
2. Preheat Ninja Foodi by pressing the "GRILL" option and setting it to "MED" and timer to 18 minutes
3. Let it preheat until you hear a beep
4. Arrange diced steak over grill grate, lock lid and cook for 9 minutes
5. Flip and cook for 9 minutes more
6. Take a blender and blend in salsa, cilantro
7. Serve with grilled steak, with blended salsa, tomato, and avocado
8. Enjoy!

<u>Nutritional Values (Per Serving)</u>
Calories: 520 Fat: 31 g Saturated Fat: 9 g Carbohydrates: 38 g Fiber: 2 g Sodium: 301 mg Protein: 41 g

All-Time Pineapple Steak

Prep Time: 5-10 minutes
Cooking Time: 8 minutes
Number of Servings: 5

Ingredients:

- ½ medium pineapple, cored and diced
- 1 jalapeno pepper, seeded and stemmed, diced
- 1 medium red onion, diced
- 4 fillet mignon steak, (6-8 ounces)
- 1 tablespoon canola oil
- Salt and pepper to taste
- 1 tablespoon lime juice
- ¼ cup cilantro, chopped
- Chili powder and ground coriander

Method:

1. Rub fillets with oil all over the steak and season with salt and pepper
2. Set you Ninja Foodi to GRILL mode and select HIGH, adjust the timer to 8 minutes
3. Let it preheat until you hear a beep
4. Arrange fillets over grill grate, cook for 4m minutes
5. Flip and cook for 4 minutes more until internal temperature reaches 125 degrees F
6. Take a bowl and add pineapple, onion, jalapeno
7. Add lime juice, cilantro, chili powder, coriander, and mix
8. Serve fillets with pineapple mix and serve
9. Enjoy!

<u>Nutritional Values (Per Serving)</u>

Calories: 536 Fat: 22 g Saturated Fat: 7 g Carbohydrates: 21 g Fiber: 4 g Sodium: 286 mg Protein: 58 g

Rosemary Anchovy Lamb

Prep Time: 5-10 min.
Cooking Time: 95 min.
Number of Servings: 8

Ingredients:
- 2 cups chicken broth
- 6 anchovies fillets, chopped
- 2 teaspoons olive oil
- 4 pounds bone-in lamb shoulder
- 1 rosemary sprig
- 1 teaspoon dried oregano
- 1 teaspoon garlic, minced
- Salt, to taste preference

Method:
1. Take Ninja Foodi multi-cooker, arrange it over a cooking platform, and open the top lid.
2. In the pot, add the oil; Select "SEAR/SAUTÉ" mode and select "MD: HI" pressure level. Press "STOP/START." After about 4-5 minutes, the oil will start simmering.
3. Add the lamb shoulder and stir-cook for about 2-3 minutes to brown evenly. Set aside.
4. In the pot, add the broth, anchovies, and garlic puree. Add the lamb shoulder on top and sprinkle with oregano, rosemary, and salt. Stir the mixture.
5. Seal the multi-cooker by locking it with the pressure lid; ensure to keep the pressure release valve locked/sealed.
6. Select "PRESSURE" mode and select the "HI" pressure level. Then, set timer to 90 minutes and press "STOP/START"; it will start the cooking process by building up inside pressure.
7. When the timer goes off, naturally release inside pressure for about 8-10 minutes. Then, quick-release pressure by adjusting the pressure valve to the VENT.
8. Open the lid, slice the lamb into small pieces, and serve warm.

Nutritional Values (Per Serving):
Calories: 456 Fat: 19.5g Saturated Fat: 2g Trans Fat: 0g Carbohydrates: 3g Fiber: 0g Sodium: 958mg Protein: 48g

Rosemary And Gold Potatoes Chop

Prep Time: 10 minutes
Cooking Time: 25 minutes
Number of Servings: 4

Ingredients:
- 1 yellow onion, chopped
- 2 tablespoons rosemary, chopped
- 4 pork chops
- 1-pound gold potatoes halved
- 1 tablespoon olive oil
- Pepper and salt to taste

Method:
1. Take your baking pan and grease with cooking spray, add ingredients and mix them
2. Pre-heat Ninja Foodi by pressing the "ROAST" option and setting it to "370 degrees F" and timer to 25 minutes
3. Let it pre-heat until you hear a beep
4. Transfer baking dish to your Ninja Foodi Grill and let it bake until the timer runs out
5. Serve and enjoy once ready!

Nutritional Values (Per Serving)

Calories: 186 Fat: 6 g Saturated Fat: 2 g Carbohydrates: 21 g Fiber: 3 g Sodium: 885 mg Protein: 10 g

Authentic Asian Apple Steak

Prep Time: 10 minutes
Cooking Time: 15-20 minutes
Number of Servings: 4

Ingredients:
- 3 tablespoons sesame oil
- 3 tablespoons brown sugar
- 1 and ½ pounds beef tips
- 4 garlic cloves, minced
- ½ apple, peeled and grated
- 1/3 cup soy sauce
- 1 teaspoon ground black pepper
- Salt and pepper to taste

Method:
1. Take your mixing bowl and add garlic, apple, sesame oil, sugar, soy sauce, pepper and salt
2. Add remaining ingredients and mix well
3. Add beef and coat for 1-2 hours, let it marinate
4. Pre-heat Ninja Foodi by pressing the GRILL" option and set it to "MED" and timer to 14 minutes
5. Let it pre-heat until you hear a beep
6. Arrange beef over grill grate, lock lid and cook for until timer reads 11 minutes
7. After that, cook until the internal temperature reaches 145 degrees F, cook for 3 minutes more if needed
8. Serve and enjoy!

Nutritional Values (Per Serving)
Calories: 517 Fat: 29 g Saturated Fat: 5 g Carbohydrates: 16 g Fiber: 4 g Sodium: 1198 mg Protein: 36 g

Lamb And Garlic Sauce

Prep Time: 10 minutes

Cooking Time: 5-10 minutes

Number of Servings: 4

Ingredients:
- 1 garlic bulb
- 3 tablespoons olive oil
- 1 tablespoon fresh oregano, chopped
- Fresh ground black pepper
- 8 lamb chops

Method:
1. Pre-heat Ninja Foodi by pressing the "AIR CRISP" option and setting it to "392 Degrees F" and timer to 10 minutes
2. Take a garlic bulb and coat with olive oil
3. Roast bulb for 12 minutes in Ninja Foodi Grill
4. Take a bowl and add salt, olive oil, and pepper
5. Coat lamb chops with a ½ tablespoon of herb/oil mix and lets it marinate for 5 minutes
6. Remove the bulb from coking tray and add lamb to the Grill, cook for 5 minutes
7. Squeeze garlic clove between your thumb and index finger over the herb oil mix, season with salt and pepper
8. Serve the lamb chops with garlic sauce
9. Enjoy!

Nutritional Values (Per Serving)
Calories: 370 Fat: 35 g Saturated Fat: 6 g Carbohydrates: 1 g Fiber: 0.3 g Sodium: 160 mg Protein: 15 g

Chimichurri Sauce Steak

Prep Time: 10 minutes
Cooking Time: 10 minutes
Number of Servings: 4

Ingredients:
- 16 ounces skirt steak

Chimichurri Sauce
- 1 cup parsley, chopped
- ¼ cup mint, chopped
- 2 tablespoons oregano, chopped
- 3 garlic cloves, chopped
- 1 teaspoon crushed red pepper
- 1 tablespoon cumin, grounded
- 1 teaspoon cayenne pepper
- 2 teaspoons smoked paprika
- 1 teaspoon salt
- ¼ teaspoon pepper
- ¾ cup olive oil
- 3 tablespoons red wine vinegar

Method:
1. Take a bowl and mix all of the ingredients listed under Chimichurri section and mix them well
2. Cut the steak into 2 pieces of 8-ounce portions
3. Take a resealable bag and add ¼ cup of Chimichurri alongside the steak pieces and shake them to ensure that steak is coated well
4. Allow it to chill in your fridge for 2-24 hours
5. Remove the steak from the fridge 30 minutes before cooking
6. Pre-heat Ninja Foodi by pressing the "AIR CRISP" option and setting it to "390 Degrees F" and timer to 10 minutes
7. Transfer the steak to your Ninja Foodi Grill and cook for about 8-10 minutes if you are looking for a medium-rare finish
8. Garnish with 2 tablespoons of Chimichurri sauce and enjoy!

<u>Nutritional Values (Per Serving)</u>

Calories: 300 Fat: 18 g Saturated Fat: 4 g Carbohydrates: 80 g Fiber: 4 g Sodium: 415 mg Protein: 13 g

Chimichurri Sauce Steak

Prep Time: 10 minutes
Cooking Time: 10 minutes
Number of Servings: 4

Ingredients:

- 16 ounces skirt steak

Chimichurri Sauce

- 1 cup parsley, chopped
- ¼ cup mint, chopped
- 2 tablespoons oregano, chopped
- 3 garlic cloves, chopped
- 1 teaspoon crushed red pepper
- 1 tablespoon cumin, grounded
- 1 teaspoon cayenne pepper
- 2 teaspoons smoked paprika
- 1 teaspoon salt
- ¼ teaspoon pepper
- ¾ cup olive oil
- 3 tablespoons red wine vinegar

Method:

1. Take a bowl and mix all of the ingredients listed under Chimichurri section and mix them well
2. Cut the steak into 2 pieces of 8-ounce portions
3. Take a resealable bag and add ¼ cup of Chimichurri alongside the steak pieces and shake them to ensure that steak is coated well
4. Allow it to chill in your fridge for 2-24 hours
5. Remove the steak from the fridge 30 minutes before cooking
6. Pre-heat Ninja Foodi by pressing the "AIR CRISP" option and setting it to "390 Degrees F" and timer to 10 minutes
7. Transfer the steak to your Ninja Foodi Grill and cook for about 8-10 minutes if you are looking for a medium-rare finish
8. Garnish with 2 tablespoons of Chimichurri sauce and enjoy!

<u>Nutritional Values (Per Serving)</u>

Calories: 300 Fat: 18 g Saturated Fat: 4 g Carbohydrates: 80 g Fiber: 4 g Sodium: 415 mg Protein: 13 g

Lamb And Garlic Sauce

Prep Time: 10 minutes

Cooking Time: 5-10 minutes

Number of Servings: 4

Ingredients:
- 1 garlic bulb
- 3 tablespoons olive oil
- 1 tablespoon fresh oregano, chopped
- Fresh ground black pepper
- 8 lamb chops

Method:
1. Pre-heat Ninja Foodi by pressing the "AIR CRISP" option and setting it to "392 Degrees F" and timer to 10 minutes
2. Take a garlic bulb and coat with olive oil
3. Roast bulb for 12 minutes in Ninja Foodi Grill
4. Take a bowl and add salt, olive oil, and pepper
5. Coat lamb chops with a ½ tablespoon of herb/oil mix and lets it marinate for 5 minutes
6. Remove the bulb from coking tray and add lamb to the Grill, cook for 5 minutes
7. Squeeze garlic clove between your thumb and index finger over the herb oil mix, season with salt and pepper
8. Serve the lamb chops with garlic sauce
9. Enjoy!

<u>Nutritional Values (Per Serving)</u>
Calories: 370 Fat: 35 g Saturated Fat: 6 g Carbohydrates: 1 g Fiber: 0.3 g Sodium: 160 mg Protein: 15 g

Fine Onion Roasted Beef

Prep Time: 5-10 minutes
Cooking Time: 30 minutes
Number of Servings: 6

Ingredients:
- 2 sticks celery, sliced
- 1 bulb garlic, peeled and crushed
- Bunch of herbs
- 2 pounds topside beef
- 2 medium onion, chopped
- Salt and pepper to taste
- 1 tablespoon butter
- 3 tablespoons olive oil

Method:
1. Take a mixing bowl and add listed ingredients, combine well with each other
2. Pre-heat Ninja Foodi by pressing the "ROAST" option and setting it to "380 Degrees F" and timer to 30 minutes
3. Let it pre-heat until you hear a beep
4. Arrange bowl mixture in your Nina Foodi Pan, cook until the timer reads zero
5. Serve and enjoy!

Nutritional Values (Per Serving)

Calories: 320 Fat: 17 g Saturated Fat: 3 g Carbohydrates: 11 g Fiber: 2 g Sodium: 632 mg Protein: 31 g

Green Pesto Ala Beef

Prep Time: 10 minutes
Cooking Time: 14 minutes
Number of Servings: 4

Ingredients:

- 4 beef (6 ounces) tenderloin steak
- 10 ounces baby spinach, chopped
- 4 cups penne pasta, uncooked
- 4 cups grape tomatoes, halved
- ½ cup walnuts, chopped
- 2/3 cup pesto
- ½ cup feta cheese, crumbled
- ½ teaspoon salt
- ½ teaspoon pepper

Method:

1. Prepare the pasta as per the given instructions on the pack
2. Drain and rinse, then keep this pasta aside
3. Season the tenderloin steaks with salt and pepper
4. Preheat Ninja Foodi by pressing the "GRILL" option and setting it to "HIGH" for 7 minutes
5. Once it preheats until you hear a beep, open the lid
6. Place the steaks in the grill grate and cook for 7 minutes
7. Flip it and cook for 7 minutes
8. Take a bowl and toss the pasta with spinach, tomatoes, walnuts, and pesto
9. Garnish with cheese
10. Serve and enjoy!

<u>Nutritional Values (Per Serving)</u>

Calories: 361 Fat: 5 g Saturated Fat: 1 g Carbohydrates: 16 g Fiber: 4 g Sodium: 269 mg Protein: 33 g

Bourbon Flavored Pork Chops

Prep Time: 5-10 minutes
Cooking Time: 20 minutes
Number of Servings: 5

Ingredients:

- 4 boneless pork chops
- Salt and pepper
- ¼ cup apple cider vinegar
- ¼ cup of soy sauce
- 3 tablespoons Worcestershire sauce
- 2 cups ketchup
- ¾ cup bourbon
- 1 cup packed brown sugar
- ½ tablespoon dry mustard powder

Method:

1. Set you Ninja Foodi to GRILL mode and select MED, adjust the timer to 15 minutes
2. Let it preheat until you hear a beep
3. Arrange pork chops over grill grate, lock lid
4. Cook for 8 minutes, flip and cook for 2 minutes more If needed
5. Take a saucepan and heat remaining ingredients until the sauce boils
6. Lower heat to low and simmer for 20 minutes
7. Serve pork chops with the sauce
8. Enjoy!

Nutritional Values (Per Serving)

Calories: 346 Fat: 13 g Saturated Fat: 4 g Carbohydrates: 27 g Fiber: 0.4 g Sodium: 1324 mg Protein: 27 g

Chapter 5: Fish And Seafood Recipes

Mustard-y Crisped Up Cod

Prep Time: 5-10 minutes
Cooking Time: 10 minutes
Number of Servings: 3

Ingredients:
- 1 large whole egg
- 1 teaspoon Dijon mustard
- ½ cup bread crumbs
- 1-pound cod filets
- ¼ cup all-purpose flour
- 1 tablespoon dried parsley
- 1 teaspoon paprika
- ½ teaspoon pepper

Method:
1. Take fish fillets and slice them into 1 inch wide strips
2. Take a mixing bowl and whisk in eggs, add mustard and combine well
3. Add flour in another bowl
4. Take another bowl and add bread crumbs, dried parsley, paprika, black pepper and combine well
5. Coat strips with flour, then coat with egg mix, coat with crumbs at last
6. Preheat Ninja Foodi by pressing the "AIR CRISP" option and setting it to "390 Degrees F" and timer to 10 minutes
7. Let it preheat until you hear a beep
8. Arrange strips directly inside basket, lock lid and cook until the timer runs out
9. Serve and enjoy!

Nutritional Values (Per Serving)
Calories: 200 Fat: 4 g Saturated Fat: 1 g Carbohydrates: 17 g Fiber: 1 g Sodium: 214 mg Protein: 24 g

Daring Spicy Grilled Shrimp

Prep Time: 5-10 minutes
Cooking Time: 6 minutes
Number of Servings: 4

Ingredients:
- 1 teaspoon garlic salt
- ½ teaspoon black pepper
- 1 tablespoon paprika
- 1 tablespoon garlic powder
- 2 tablespoons olive oil
- 1-pound jumbo shrimps, peeled and deveined
- 2 tablespoons brown sugar

Method:
1. Take a mixing bowl and add listed ingredients to mix well
2. Let it chill and marinate for 30-60 minutes
3. Preheat Ninja Foodi by pressing the "GRILL" option and setting it to "MED" and timer to 6 minutes
4. Let it preheat until you hear a beep
5. Arrange prepared shrimps over grill grate, lock lid and cook for 3 minutes, flip and cook for 3 minutes more
6. Serve and enjoy!

Nutritional Values (Per Serving)
Calories: 370 Fat: 27 g Saturated Fat: 3 g Carbohydrates: 23 g Fiber: 8 g Sodium: 182 mg Protein: 6 g

Awesome Shrimp Roast

Prep Time: 5-10 minutes
Cooking Time: 7 minutes
Number of Servings: 2

Ingredients:
- 3 tablespoons chipotle in adobo sauce, minced
- ¼ teaspoon salt
- ¼ cup BBQ sauce
- ½ orange, juiced
- ½ pound large shrimps

Method:
1. Take a mixing bowl and add all ingredients, mix well
2. Keep it on the side
3. Preheat Ninja Foodi by pressing the "ROAST" option and setting it to "400 Degrees F" and timer to 7 minutes
4. Let it preheat until you hear a beep
5. Arrange shrimps over Grill Grate and lock lid, cook until the timer runs out
6. Serve and enjoy!

<u>Nutritional Values (Per Serving)</u>

Calories: 173 Fat: 2 g Saturated Fat: 0.5 g Carbohydrates: 21 g Fiber: 2 g Sodium: 1143 mg Protein: 17 g

Salmon And Dill Sauce Meal

Prep Time: 10 minutes
Cooking Time: 20-25 minutes
Number of Servings: 4

Ingredients:
- 4 salmon, each of 6 ounces
- 2 teaspoons olive oil
- 1 pinch salt

Dill Sauce
- ½ cup non-fat Greek Yogurt
- ½ cup sour cream
- Pinch of salt
- 2 tablespoons dill, chopped

Method:
1. Pre-heat Ninja Foodi by pressing the "AIR CRISP" option and setting it to "270 Degrees F" and timer to 25 minutes
2. Wait until the appliance beeps
3. Drizzle cut pieces of salmon with 1 teaspoon olive oil
4. Season with salt
5. Take the cooking basket out and transfer salmon to basket, cook for 20-23 minutes
6. Take a bowl and add sour cream, salt, chopped dill, yogurt and mix well to prepare the dill sauce
7. Serve cooked salmon by pouring the sauce all over
8. Garnish with chopped dill and enjoy!

Nutritional Values (Per Serving)
Calories: 600 Fat: 45 g Saturated Fat: 6 g Carbohydrates: 5 g Fiber: 2 g Sodium: 422 mg Protein: 60 g

Spicy Cajun Shrimp

Prep Time: 10 minutes
Cooking Time: 7 minutes
Number of Servings: 4

Ingredients:
- 1 and ¼ pound tiger shrimp, about 16-20 pieces
- ¼ teaspoon cayenne pepper
- ½ teaspoon old bay seasoning
- ¼ teaspoon smoked paprika
- 1 pinch of salt
- 1 tablespoon olive oil

Method:
1. Pre-heat Ninja Foodi by pressing the "AIR CRISP" option and setting it to "390 Degrees F" and timer to 10 minutes
2. Take a mixing bowl and add ingredients (except shrimp), mix well
3. Dip the shrimp into spice mixture and oil
4. Transfer the prepared shrimp to your Ninja Foodi Grill cooking basket and cook for 5 minutes
5. Serve and enjoy!

Nutritional Values (Per Serving)
Calories: 170 Fat: 2 g Saturated Fat: 0.5 g Carbohydrates: 5 g Fiber: 2 g Sodium: 1236 mg Protein: 23 g

Subtly Roasted BBQ Shrimp

Prep Time: 5-10 minutes
Cooking Time: 7 minutes
Number of Servings: 2

Ingredients:
- 3 tablespoons chipotle in adobo sauce, minced
- ¼ teaspoon salt
- ¼ cup BBQ sauce
- ½ orange, juiced
- ½ pound large shrimps

Method:
1. Take a mixing bowl and add all ingredients, mix well
2. Keep it on the side
3. Pre-heat Ninja Foodi by pressing the "ROAST" option and setting it to "400 Degrees F" and timer to 7 minutes
4. Let it pre-heat until you hear a beep
5. Arrange shrimps over Grill Grate and lock lid, cook until the timer runs out
6. Serve and enjoy!

Nutritional Values (Per Serving)

Calories: 173 Fat: 2 g Saturated Fat: 0.5 g Carbohydrates: 21 g Fiber: 2 g Sodium: 1143 mg Protein: 17 g

Coho Glazed Salmon

Prep Time: 10 minutes
Cooking Time: 25 minutes
Number of Servings: 4

Ingredients:

- 1-2 coho salmon filets
- 1 cup of water
- ¼ cup of soy sauce
- ¼ cup brown sugar
- 1 tablespoon honey
- 1 and ½ tablespoons ginger roots, minced
- ½ teaspoon white pepper
- 2 tablespoons cornstarch
- ¼ cup of cold water

Method:

1. Insert the grill grate and close the hood
2. Preheat Ninja Foodi by pressing the "GRILL" option and setting it to "HIGH" for 15 minutes
3. Take a medium saucepan over medium heat, combine sauce ingredients(except salmon, cornstarch and cold water) and bring to a low boil
4. Then add cornstarch and water in another bowl, whisk cornstarch mixture slowly into sauce until it thickens
5. Add one chunk of pecan wood to the hot coal of your grill
6. Brush sauce onto the salmon filet
7. Place on the grill grate, then close the hood
8. Cook for 15 minutes
9. Brush the salmon with another coat of sauce
10. Close the lid and cook for 10 minutes more
11. Serve and enjoy!

<u>Nutritional Values (Per Serving)</u>

Calories: 163 Fat: 0 g Saturated Fat: 0 g Carbohydrates: 15 g Fiber: 3 g Sodium: 456 mg Protein: 0 g

Swordfish With Caper Sauce

Prep Time: 10 minutes
Cooking Time: 8 minutes
Number of Servings: 4

Ingredients:

- 4 swordfish steaks, about 1-inch thick
- 4 tablespoons unsalted butter
- 1 lemon, sliced into 8 slices
- 1 tablespoon lemon juice
- 1 tablespoon extra-virgin olive oil
- 2 tablespoons capers, drained
- Sea salt
- Black pepper, freshly grounded

Method:

1. Take a large shallow bowl and whisk together the lemon juice and oil
2. Season with swordfish steaks with salt and pepper on each side, place in the oil mixture
3. Turn to coat both sides and refrigerate for 15 minutes
4. Insert the grill grate and close the hood
5. Preheat Ninja Foodi by pressing the "GRILL" option at and setting it to "MAX" and timer to 8 minutes
6. Let it preheat until you hear a beep
7. Arrange the swordfish over the grill grate, lock lid and cook for 9 minutes
8. Place a medium saucepan over medium heat and melt butter
9. Add the lemon slices and capers to the pan and cook for 1 minute
10. Then turn off the heat
11. Remove the swordfish from the grill and serve with caper sauce over it
12. Enjoy!

Nutritional Values (Per Serving)

Calories: 472 Fat: 31 g Saturated Fat: 6 g Carbohydrates: 2 g Fiber: 0.5 g Sodium: 540 mg Protein: 48 g

Chapter 6: Desserts

Rummy Pineapple Sunday

Prep Time: 10 minutes
Cooking Time: 8 minutes
Number of Servings: 4

Ingredients:
- ½ cup dark rum
- ½ cup packed brown sugar
- 1 teaspoon ground cinnamon, plus more for garnish
- 1 pineapple cored and sliced
- Vanilla ice cream, for serving

Method:
1. Take a large-sized bowl and add rum, sugar, cinnamon
2. Add pineapple slices, arrange them in the layer. Coat mixture then let them soak for 5 minutes, per side
3. Preheat Ninja Foodi by pressing the "GRILL" option and setting it to "MAX" and timer to 8 minutes
4. let it preheat until you hear a beep
5. Strain extra rum sauce from pineapple
6. Transfer prepared fruit in grill grate in a single layer, press down fruit and lock lid
7. Grill for 6-8 minutes without flipping, work in batches if needed
8. Once done, remove and top each pineapple ring with a scoop of ice cream, sprinkle cinnamon and serve
9. Enjoy!

Nutritional Values (Per Serving)
Calories: 240 Fat: 4 g Saturated Fat: 2 g Carbohydrates: 43 g Fiber: 3 g Sodium: 32 mg Protein: 2 g

Chapter 6: Desserts

Rummy Pineapple Sunday

Prep Time: 10 minutes
Cooking Time: 8 minutes
Number of Servings: 4

Ingredients:
- ½ cup dark rum
- ½ cup packed brown sugar
- 1 teaspoon ground cinnamon, plus more for garnish
- 1 pineapple cored and sliced
- Vanilla ice cream, for serving

Method:
1. Take a large-sized bowl and add rum, sugar, cinnamon
2. Add pineapple slices, arrange them in the layer. Coat mixture then let them soak for 5 minutes, per side
3. Preheat Ninja Foodi by pressing the "GRILL" option and setting it to "MAX" and timer to 8 minutes
4. let it preheat until you hear a beep
5. Strain extra rum sauce from pineapple
6. Transfer prepared fruit in grill grate in a single layer, press down fruit and lock lid
7. Grill for 6-8 minutes without flipping, work in batches if needed
8. Once done, remove and top each pineapple ring with a scoop of ice cream, sprinkle cinnamon and serve
9. Enjoy!

Nutritional Values (Per Serving)
Calories: 240 Fat: 4 g Saturated Fat: 2 g Carbohydrates: 43 g Fiber: 3 g Sodium: 32 mg Protein: 2 g

Swordfish With Caper Sauce

Prep Time: 10 minutes
Cooking Time: 8 minutes
Number of Servings: 4

Ingredients:

- 4 swordfish steaks, about 1-inch thick
- 4 tablespoons unsalted butter
- 1 lemon, sliced into 8 slices
- 1 tablespoon lemon juice
- 1 tablespoon extra-virgin olive oil
- 2 tablespoons capers, drained
- Sea salt
- Black pepper, freshly grounded

Method:

1. Take a large shallow bowl and whisk together the lemon juice and oil
2. Season with swordfish steaks with salt and pepper on each side, place in the oil mixture
3. Turn to coat both sides and refrigerate for 15 minutes
4. Insert the grill grate and close the hood
5. Preheat Ninja Foodi by pressing the "GRILL" option at and setting it to "MAX" and timer to 8 minutes
6. Let it preheat until you hear a beep
7. Arrange the swordfish over the grill grate, lock lid and cook for 9 minutes
8. Place a medium saucepan over medium heat and melt butter
9. Add the lemon slices and capers to the pan and cook for 1 minute
10. Then turn off the heat
11. Remove the swordfish from the grill and serve with caper sauce over it
12. Enjoy!

Nutritional Values (Per Serving)

Calories: 472 Fat: 31 g Saturated Fat: 6 g Carbohydrates: 2 g Fiber: 0.5 g Sodium: 540 mg Protein: 48 g

Marshmallow Banana Boat

Prep Time: 19 minutes
Cooking Time: 6 minutes
Number of Servings: 4

Ingredients:
- 4 ripe bananas
- 1 cup mini marshmallows
- ½ cup of chocolate chips
- ½ cup peanut butter chips

Method:
1. Slice a banana lengthwise, keeping its peel. Make sure to not cut all the way through
2. Use your hands to open banana peel like a book, revealing the inside of a banana
3. Divide marshmallow, chocolate chips, peanut butter among bananas, stuffing them inside
4. Preheat Ninja Foodi by pressing the "GRILL" option and setting it to "MEDIUM" and timer to 6 minutes
5. let it preheat until you hear a beep
6. Transfer banana to Grill Grate and lock lid, cook for 4-6 minutes until chocolate melts and bananas are toasted
7. Serve and enjoy!

Nutritional Values (Per Serving)
Calories: 505 Fat: 18 g Saturated Fat: 13 g Carbohydrates: 82 g Fiber: 6 g Sodium: 103 mg Protein: 10 g

Fiery Cajun Eggplant Dish

Prep Time: 5-10 minutes
Cooking Time: 12 minutes
Number of Servings: 4

Ingredients:
- 2 tablespoons lime juice
- 3 teaspoons Cajun seasoning
- 2 small eggplants, cut into slices
- ¼ cup olive oil

Method:
1. Coat eggplant slices with oil, lemon juice, and Cajun seasoning
2. Take your Ninja Foodi Grill and press "GRILL" and set to "MED" mode, set the timer to 10 minutes
3. Let it preheat
4. Arrange eggplants over grill grate, lock lid and cook for 5 minutes
5. Flip and cook for 5 minutes more
6. Serve and enjoy!

Nutritional Values (Per Serving)
Calories: 362 Fat: 11 g Saturated Fat: 3 g Carbohydrates: 16 g Fiber: 1 g Sodium: 694 mg Protein: 8 g

Granola Flavored Healthy Muffin

Prep Time: 10 minutes
Cooking Time: 15-20 minutes
Number of Servings: 4

Ingredients:
- 3 ounces plain granola
- 3 handful of cooked vegetables of your choice
- ¼ cup of coconut milk
- A handful of thyme diced
- 1 tablespoon coriander
- Salt and pepper to taste

Method:
1. Preheat Ninja Foodi by pressing the "AIR CRISP" option and setting it to "352 Degrees F" and timer to 20 minutes
2. Take a mixing bowl and add cooked vegetables
3. Take an immersion blender and whiz granola until you have a breadcrumb-like texture
4. Add coconut milk to the granola and add **veggies**
5. Mix well into muffin/ball shapes
6. Transfer them to preheated Ninja Foodi Grill and cook for 20 minutes
7. Serve and enjoy once done!

<u>Nutritional Values (Per Serving)</u>
Calories: 140 Fat: 10 g Saturated Fat: 3 g Carbohydrates: 14 g Fiber: 4 g Sodium: 215 mg Protein: 2 g

Chapter 7: Snacks And Appetizers Recipes

Summer Squash With Garlic

Prep Time: 15 minutes
Cooking Time: 15 minutes
Number of Servings: 4

Ingredients:
- ½ cup vegetable oil + 3 tablespoons
- ¼ cup white wine vinegar
- 1 garlic clove, grated
- 2 summer squash, sliced lengthwise about ¼ inch thick
- 1 red onion, peeled and cut into wedges
- Salt and pepper to taste
- 1 pack 8 ounces crumbled feta cheese
- Red pepper flakes

Method:
1. Take a small-sized bowl and whisk in ½ cup oil, vinegar, garlic and keep it on the side
2. Take a large-sized bowl and toss squash, onion with remaining 3 tablespoons of oil and coat them well
3. Season with salt and pepper
4. Preheat Ninja Foodi by pressing the "GRILL" option and setting it to "MAX" and timer to 10 minutes
5. let it preheat until you hear a beep
6. Arrange squash onions on the grill grate, lock hood and cook for 6 minutes, open hood and flip squash
7. Lock lid and cook for 6-9 minutes more
8. Once the veggies are cooked to your desired doneness, remove from grill and arrange them on a large platter
9. Top with cheese and a drizzle of dressing, sprinkle red pepper flakes
10. Let is stand for 15 minutes
11. Serve and enjoy!

Nutritional Values (Per Serving)
Calories: 521 Fat: 50 g Saturated Fat: 16 g Carbohydrates: 11 g Fiber: 2 g Sodium: 797 mg Protein: 10 g

Italian Oregano Squash

Prep Time: 5-10 minutes
Cooking Time: 16 minutes
Number of Servings: 4

Ingredients:
- 1 medium butternut squash, peeled, seeded and cut into ½ inch slices
- 1 teaspoon dried thyme
- ½ teaspoon salt
- 1 tablespoon olive oil
- 1 and ½ teaspoons dried oregano
- ¼ teaspoon black pepper

Method:
1. Take a mixing bowl and add slices alongside other ingredients, mix well
2. Preheat Ninja Foodi by pressing the "GRILL" option and setting it to "MED" and timer to 16 minutes
3. let it preheat until you hear a beep
4. Arrange squash slices over the grill grate
5. Cook for 8 minutes, flip and cook for 8 minutes more
6. Serve and enjoy!

Nutritional Values (Per Serving)
Calories: 238 Fat: 12 g Saturated Fat: 2 g Carbohydrates: 36 g Fiber: 3 g Sodium: 128 mg Protein: 15 g

Elegant Pumpkin Seeds

Prep Time: 10 minutes

Cooking Time: 35 minutes

Number of Servings: 2

Ingredients:

- 1 and ½ cups pumpkin seeds
- Olive oil as needed
- 1 and ½ teaspoons salt
- 1 teaspoon smoked paprika

Method:

1. Pre-heat Ninja Foodi by pressing the "AIR CRISP" option and setting it to "350 Degrees F" and timer to 35 minutes
2. let it pre-heat until you hear a beep
3. Cut pumpkin and scrape out seeds and flesh
4. Separate flesh from seeds and rinse the seeds under cold water
5. Bring 2 quarter of salted water to boil and add seeds, boil for 10 minutes
6. Drain seeds and spread them on a kitchen towel
7. Dry for 20 minutes
8. Take a bowl and add seeds, smoked paprika, and olive oil
9. Season with salt and transfer to your Air Fryer cooking basket
10. Cook for 35 minutes, enjoy it!

<u>Nutritional Values (Per Serving)</u>
Calories: 270 Fat: 21 g Saturated Fat: 4 g Carbohydrates: 4 g Fiber: 2 g Sodium: 126 mg Protein: 12 g

Hearty Banana Fritters

Prep Time: 10 minutes
Cooking Time: 16 minutes
Number of Servings: 6

Ingredients:
- 1 medium butternut squash
- 2 teaspoons cumin seeds
- 1 large pinch chili flakes
- 1 tablespoon olive oil
- 1 and ½ ounces pine nuts
- 1 small bunch fresh coriander, chopped

Method:
1. Pre-heat Ninja Foodi by pressing the "AIR CRISP" option and setting it to "340 Degrees F" and timer to 16 minutes
2. let it pre-heat until you hear a beep
3. Take a bowl and add salt, sesame seeds, water and mix them well until a nice batter form
4. Coat the bananas with the flour mixture and transfer them to the Ninja Foodi Grill Basket
5. Cook for 8 minutes
6. Enjoy!

Nutritional Values (Per Serving)

Calories: 240 Fat: 10 g Saturated Fat: 4 g Carbohydrates: 30 g Fiber: 2 g Sodium: 22 mg Protein: 5 g

Cool Avocado Fries

Prep Time: 15 minutes
Cooking Time: 15-20 minutes
Number of Servings: 6

Ingredients:
- ½ cup breadcrumbs
- ½ teaspoon salt
- 1 Hass avocado, peeled, pitted and sliced
- Aquafaba from one bean can (bean liquid)

Method:
1. Pre-heat Ninja Foodi by pressing the "AIR CRISP" option and setting it to "390 Degrees F" and timer to 10 minutes
2. let it pre-heat until you hear a beep
3. Take a shallow bowl and add breadcrumbs, salt
4. Pour aquafaba in another bowl, dredge avocado slices in aquafaba and then into the crumbs to get a nice coating
5. Arrange them in a single layer in your Ninja Foodi Cooking basket, don't overlap
6. Let them cook for 10 minutes, makings sure to shake after 5 minutes
7. Serve and enjoy!

<u>Nutritional Values (Per Serving)</u>

Calories: 340 Fat: 14 g Saturated Fat: 4 g Carbohydrates: 30 g Fiber: 2 g Sodium: 91 mg Protein: 23 g

Fully Seasoned Broccoli Delight

Prep Time: 15 minutes
Cooking Time: 10 minutes
Number of Servings: 4

Ingredients:
- 1 pound broccoli, cut into florets
- ¼ teaspoon turmeric powder
- 1 tablespoon chickpea flour
- 2 tablespoons yogurt
- ¼ teaspoon spice mix
- ½ teaspoon red chili powder
- ½ teaspoon salt

Method:
1. Wash florets well
2. Take a bowl and add listed ingredients except for florets
3. Add broccoli and combine well, let it seat for 30 minutes
4. Let the Ninja Foodi Preheat in Air Crisp mode,
5. Once you hear a beep, transfer to Ninja Foodi Grill and cook on AIR CRISP mode for 10 minutes at 390 degrees F
6. Serve and enjoy!

<u>Nutritional Values (Per Serving)</u>

Calories: 111 Fat: 2 g Saturated Fat: 1 g Carbohydrates: 12 g Fiber: 1 g Sodium: 024 mg Protein: 7 g

www.ingramcontent.com/pod-product-compliance
Lightning Source LLC
Chambersburg PA
CBHW081126080526
44587CB00021B/3769